Cumbria
TRUE TO THE LAND

The Hill Farming Photographs of Tony Hopkins

HALSGROVE

First published in Great Britain in 2004

British Library Cataloguing-in-Publication Data
A CIP record for this title is available from the British Library

ISBN 1 84114 394 4

HALSGROVE

Halsgrove House
Lower Moor Way
Tiverton, Devon EX16 6SS
Tel: 01884 243242
Fax: 01884 243325
email: sales@halsgrove.com
website: www.halsgrove.com

Printed by D'Auria Industrie Grafiche Spa, Italy

Contents

Introduction Forever Changes   5

1 Tip Fair   13

2 Fit for the Fell   23

3 The Golden Fleece   35

4 Wasdale Gather   45

5 Cattle Drives   63

6 Hay and Hard Times   79

7 Work in the Woods   97

8 Watendlath Gather   113

9 Patterdale Sheep Pens   125

10 Clean Money   135

11 Horse Talk   145

12 Appleby Fair   155

Getting ready for judging at Borrowdale Show. Andrew Nicholson steadying a Herdwick tup so that it shows off its best features. What makes a good tup? 'A good coat and head, and strong bones!'

Forever Changes

A summer storm was forecast. Hartside Pass was in grey mist and on the descent into Melmerby, the hedgerow ashes had already been tossed and buffeted so that leaves and branches littered the road. But the rain held off, even into the heart of the Lake District, where Skiddaw and Helvellyn were covered to their footings in cloud.

Derwentwater was sullen and Great Wood silent. I drove up the narrow twisting side-road to Watendlath and passed neither parked car nor fell-walker. When I reached Old Fold Farm and looked across the tarn to the fells, I realised I was a stranger here: it had been nine years since I had photographed Dick Richardson gathering on Black Knott.

The welcome at Old Fold was as warm as I could have wished. Dick sat back in a well-worn armchair and talked about family and friends, sheep and subsidies. When I spread out the pictures I had taken in 1995 he looked first at those of the dogs, calling his wife Margaret from the kitchen to help remember their names. Working dogs are 'curs' – collie-crosses of unlikely ancestry – but they have character. 'Fred was a good dog,' said Dick, pointing to a scruffy creature in the corner of a barn-yard picture. 'He went for miles. Miles and miles, gathering on his own. No good at short-hand though: you'd set him off in a field and he'd work into the next, and the next. But he was all right, was Fred.'

Working through the photographs it was clear how much farming had changed here in a short space of time. It would be impossible now to take pictures of hundreds of sheep being driven down to the intake,

Fell country in the Lake District: steep beds of bracken and mat-grass, and a thin scattering of sheep, on the slopes of Knott Rigg and Whiteless Pike.

because there are only half the sheep on the fells. Government policy has switched from capitation to ESA and Enhancement Scheme: in effect, local farmers are paid to have their sheep taken off the hills, to be wintered on lower ground. From November to May, the Watendlath fells are deserted. For as long as I have known the Lake District there has been talk of overgrazing and loss of bio-diversity. Dick simply shook his head, weary and wary of experts and bureaucrats. 'They've been chowin' at me for last fifteen years to drop down numbers, offering that much you can't refuse. You have to do it. And you can't get men: no labour. Nobody's coming up.'

A few minutes later, Dick's son Shaun came in with Chris Swainson and Robert Tyson. They had been gathering the Coldbarrow heath for clipping. Around the dinner table everyone pored over the pictures, recognising neighbours and telling scurrilous stories about them. The picture of Jonny Birkett 'clouting twinters' attracted special comment. 'Nobody's done that sort of thing round here for fifty years,' said someone, smiling into a mug of tea. But of course they have. Everything in the photographs is still happening somewhere in the Cumbrian hills. But only just.

Outside, the wind was whipping the tarn into shivers and swirls of spray, and leaves were dancing on the sycamores in the farmyard. When I drove out over the packhorse bridge, I stopped for a moment to look towards Coldbarrow and the shrouded fells. A stormy day, but no rain.

A Light Touch

This book is a companion to *Northumbria: True to the Land*, which was published in 2003 and contained a clutch of photographs taken in the mid 1990s, at a time when I was trying to explore my relationship with the working landscape. I had followed a career in conservation, most recently as senior manager in a National Park Authority, but was in the process of going freelance. I needed to take a step back.

Taking advantage of contacts in countryside agencies such as the National Trust and the NFU, I put together a list of farms and rural industries across the North of England where low-tech methods, sometimes old-fashioned and sometimes repackaged as environmentally-friendly or sustainable, made working processes both visual and emotionally-charged. I was interested in the day-to-day activities of people who touched the land lightly. They were not always the most communicative or gregarious of people. Some never came to the phone (if they had one), others said it would be fine for me to drop by the next morning to photograph the milking/lambing/coppicing, only to find when I got there that they had gone off to a sheep sale.

However, I soon established a working list of places to visit, mainly over a two-year period, 1994/95. I fitted the project around other commitments, setting aside odd weekends for darkroom work (on the

Derelict farmhouse near Brough. In the 1990s, out-of-the-way hills and valleys in Cumbria were full of ruins that nobody wanted. Ten years on, most have been renovated into smart and expensive homes.

dining-room table) and delivering spare copies of prints to the people in the pictures, so that I could check details and note down their stories. Over a cup of tea, often extending into dinner, I heard about the good old days and how bad things had got. What nobody knew, of course, was that in subsequent years things were to get a lot worse. Rock-bottom mart prices, BSE, foot and mouth disease and the vagaries of government grants have all played a part in undermining the confidence of the rural economy. What I had photographed was hill-farming at its high-point.

Although this book concentrates on Cumbria, I have taken the opportunity to include some other material collected at around the same time. The logic of doing this is partly that the activities illustrated add to the overall effect and help to establish a broader context, but also because in my mind the pictures rest comfortably together. I cheated in the Northumbria book too, including a sequence at Birkdale in Teesdale, which is actually situated on the Cumbrian side of Maize Beck. This time I include, among other cuckoo eggs, some of my favourite pictures taken at Sillywrea Farm, near Langley in Northumberland. Langley is only a few miles from the Cumbrian border and is to the lee of the Alston uplands, so there is a tenuous

Jonny Birkett of High Yewdale, clouting twinters. A twinter is a female sheep into its second year, but not yet strong enough to rear a lamb. To stop it from being mated, the tradition among hill farmers is to sew a patch of material onto the sheep's backside. Very few farmers still do this: the majority send their gimmers down to lower pasture, to provide them with good grazing and keep them away from the tups.

Jonny was a good hand with a darning needle, but he was using squares of bright orange blanket, which did not tone very well with the Herdwicks' fleeces and must have puzzled tourists.

Early summer, looking south across the upper Eden Valley to Cold Fell.

Late winter: a side-road to the fells, north of Alston.

case for their inclusion. However, the real reason is that when I was preparing the Northumbria book I held back most of my best Sillywrea pictures in the hopes that they would make a book on their own. That may still happen one day, but in the meantime I am making sure some more of the images see the light of day.

Shepherds' Hey

Some time in the early '90s I bought a CD of Percy Grainger music called *Shepherds' Hey*; the cover was an old photograph of a shepherd driving a cut of sheep down from Langdale. I listened to the music quite often (as English as you can get, despite the fact that he was an Australian), and I studied the cover in detail. It was, above all else, a picture I wished I could have taken myself. Over the previous few years I had written and photographed all over Cumbria, Northumberland and Durham, and I had some good images. But nothing as good or as emotionally-charged (an essential ingredient) as the one on the CD cover. I set out to produce something as good.

I also wanted to confirm my own link with the land. Everyone has farming ancestry, if they go back far enough. My list of land-labouring relatives included great-uncle Jack Morley who farmed and had a milk round at Whatstandwell in Derbyshire, and great-great-grandfather William Lines, who was shepherd to the Shuckburgh estate in Northamptonshire.

A sepia photograph of William Lines, with bushy whiskers and gnarled hands clutching his crook, has stood on our mantelpiece for many years. I sometimes look at it and wonder what his life was like, whether rural poverty was a kind of slavery. So although I was born and raised in an East Midland town I think my ancestors reached out to steady my way in the world, to take me back to the countryside. When I came to live in the North of England, I was, in a way, coming home. I was given the grace to catch up with my ancestors.

The trouble with *True to the Land* was that the material was defiantly 'retro': the past within the present. The London publishers I showed the final cut to were enthusiastic about the pictures but dubious about the market. Too regional, they said. Eventually I put everything on a shelf and, in time, left it in peace. It was only as an afterthought, several years later, that I showed it to Roly Smith of Halsgrove, when I was talking to him about a Cheviot book. To his credit, he was enthusiastic straight away, but wanted to publish either a book for Northumbria or Cumbria, but not a mixture of both. I was obliged to make a choice.

It immediately became apparent that while the Cumbria pictures were dramatic, those from Northumbria (ie Northumberland and Durham) were more varied. They represented a wide spread of rural activities: keepering, walling, ditching, digging peats. So it was the Northumbria book that was published, and I did not expect to get a second chance. When the book came out to favourable reviews, and (most importantly) kind comments from farmers, I was pleased and content.

It was only some months later, in the early summer of 2004, that Halsgrove confirmed they wanted to produce the Cumbria book too – but to a very tight deadline. Of course, I had the photographs all ready (I had decided there should be no afterthoughts, no matter how tempting), but there was no text, and very little time. My wife and I were due to move to Suffolk in July. But I could not ignore the opportunity to finish the project. There was a contract involved, not on paper but between me and my ancestors, me and the land. Hence my last trip to the Lakes, to call in and see a few of the sites I had worked on with the National Trust and the National Park, and to visit one or two farms, especially Old Fold.

Looking through the prints with Dick Richardson was a great pleasure. The batch of Cumbria photographs certainly contained the best shepherding material I had taken, hard-won over early mornings and tough climbs on to the high fells. I had achieved my original aim of doing better than the CD cover. It was a relief too to see Dick with a broadening smile on his face, re-living the dawn gather in the monochrome images. At the end of it he passed them back and said, half to himself, 'Hell, they're bloody good pictures!' and I knew that some of them were.

Gone forever. Clockwise, starting top left: Hay-making on a wet day, Lewis in the Outer Hebrides. Hay stooks drying on South Uist, Outer Hebrides. Threshing day in the Dordogne. Wheat sheaves in Normandy.

Scenes like these would have been common in Cumbria in living memory.

The photographs were taken in the mid 1990s.

Views from the A686, the dramatic trans-Pennine road. Top: East to the South Tyne Valley and Garrigill, from south of Alston. Bottom: South-west over the Eden Valley to the Lake District (hidden by low cloud). The two photographs are taken only a few miles apart, but the landscapes, farming and cultures of the areas are completely different.

Keswick Tup Fair. All eyes on the sale ring as auctioneer Adam Day gets through the business of the day. Making up the crowd (a good turn-out) are: Glen Wilkinson, Neil Hodgson, Harry Wilson, Pauline Blair, Joe Folder, Jack Bland, Peter Edmonson, Tom Robinson, William Richardson, John Hind, Pat Temple, Harry Hardesty, John Bland, Stuart Bland, Joe Relf, Stanley Jackson, John Clarke, Gordon Stagg, Kevin Wrathau, Ivor Dickinson, Vick Greg, Eric Harrison, Jeff Harrison, Andrew Nicholson, Andrew Benn, Chris Hartley, Jason Weir, Benny Steele, Betty Birkett, George Birkett, Jean Wilson and Derek Wilson.

ONE

Tip Fair

The farming year begins in the hills in November, when the tups (or 'tips') are driven out to the ewes. Sheep know their ground: they are raised to fend for themselves, to find shelter and forage for food at different times of the day and at different times of year. Thus each flock of sheep is heafted (or hefted) to a particular cut of land. Traditionally, when a hill farm changes hands the heafts are included in the sale, because it would be impossible to bring in a new flock of sheep and expect them to stay put, or survive for long, on the Pennine and Lakeland fells.

In recent years, with government encouragement (or inducement), grazing pressure on many of the Cumbrian fells has been reduced by cutting down the total number of ewes and lambs, or by taking off a proportion of them to overwinter on lowland pastures. Yet after six months away, every lamb knows its own mother, and every ewe still knows where to find the best spring bite.

Meanwhile, the tups spend their winter in the fields around the farms or in sheds. It is essential that they are kept well away from the ewes until the late autumn, to make sure that lambing is not too early or too late in the spring. Things can sometimes go awry: I once overheard two Thirlmere shepherds discussing someone in the next valley: 'Th' old bugger's lost a tip. Aye, there'll be lambs poppin' out all over the place. His neighbours 'll be savage!'

When the tups go out onto the fell they have a very busy three weeks. Clearly, a farmer expects every female sheep to be covered: if there are barren ewes at lambing time, a poor tup soon gets the blame. One of the problems with this arrangement is that young female sheep are not strong enough to raise a lamb in their second year, so the farmer has to find a way of preventing the union. These days this is done by moving them down to lowland fields, but when I was visiting remote hill farms in the mid-1990s, there were a few places where this alternative pasture was not available, so the traditional practice of sewing patches of cloth onto sheeps' back-sides was still a November ritual. In the Cheviot Hills this is called 'breeking hoggs', while in the Lake District it is called 'clouting twinters'. When the task is finished and the sheep are on the hills, farmers I have spoken to have expressed a wry or ribald sympathy for the tups, doomed to frustration.

Every autumn, hill farmers get together at sales or fairs to look over each other's stock and maybe buy a new tup, to keep their own stock robust and healthy. At one time, the annual shows and marts were the only way people could meet, so events were keenly anticipated. Now, farmers see each other at the supermarket or at the pub. Even so, families still make a day of it at the shows, and farmers always turn out for the tup sales.

In terms of total sheep numbers, the dominant breed in Cumbria is the Swaledale. To the north there are a few Blackface and Cheviot enclaves, and to the west, on the Lake District fells, there are Herdwicks. Of all the breeds on all the hills it is the Herdwick that attracts the most attention because it is so obviously different to all the others: its origins are obscure – perhaps Medieval, or Viking, or Celtic. It is the hardiest of breeds, which means it can survive the most hostile weather, but it also means it is a slow breeder and has a coarse fleece.

A century ago the Herdwick was threatened with extinction; it was saved partly through the efforts of Beatrix Potter, who invested her Peter Rabbit fortune in farms and stipulated in tenancies that the breed should be maintained. She was a doughty campaigner for the 'traditional' countryside, and she loved the Herdwick shows and sales. In her later life (as Mrs Heelis) she was known and respected locally for her prize-winning tups more than for her story-books. The National Trust – by far the biggest landowner in the Lake District – inherited most of the Heelis estate and continues to manage the tenancies.

Herdwick tups are big and solidly built. Close up, they radiate quiet disdain and brute force.

Herdwicks are still an endangered breed, if only because they are found in such a small area of the country. But every October there are tup sales, to remind everyone that the seasons are passing, and after the coming winter, there will be another harvest of lambs.

Keswick Tup Fair is no more; the Town's Field hosts a popular May Fair instead. Herdwick sales are held at an auction mart, no longer in the shadow of Skiddaw. When I spent the day at the traditional sale in 1995 everything was as it must have been the last time Beatrix Heelis took the top rosette. The sale ring was set on the level pasture a few yards away from the alder-lined banks of the River Greta. There were about a hundred people in the field altogether, and I was the only offcomer. By this time I had already got to know several of the local farmers and hired men: they ignored me (and each other) around the main pen, where there was business in progress, but around the tea van they were happy to engage in glum conversations about how bad trade was (it was always bad, even on a good day).

The auctioneer worked his way through the schedule and one by one the Herdwick tups came and went, some for £500, some for £50:

Three year old again here. What about him then? Two hundred? One hundred? Fifty pounds, thank you. Sixty, seventy, eighty... ninety, one hundred... one hundred and ten in front...one hundred and ten, one hundred and ten... Are you all done? This time he goes. Away at one hundred and ten... You bidding? All out in front of me. Come on, you haven't seen him...

I asked the owner of the champion ram what made it so special, and he said he had no idea: in his opinion it was not as good as the one that came second.

A hundred and ten bid... one-twenty... one-thirty – along the line... I'm selling him...this time he goes... one-thirty pounds, Scott Naylor!'

A sharp eye and quick-fire banter: Adam Day of Mitchell's Auctioneers. '£200. Are you all done? This time he goes. Away at 200. Are you bidding?'

Anthony Hartley with a prize-winning Herdwick ram at Keswick Tup Fair.

A line of tups ready for judging. Jean and Derek Wilson in the foreground.

Jeff Edmondson judging at Keswick Tup Fair, with help from Shaun Richardson. The teeth are always checked to see if the sheep is the correct age for its class.

Harry Hardesty and David Norman driving Herdwick ewes from a trailer into the sale pens.

Borrowdale Show, held at Rosthwaite in mid-September. The day's programme usually contains such events as Cumberland and Westmorland wrestling, a fell race, a hound trail and the judging of sheep and fell ponies.

David Norman and Gordon Stagg with time to talk: Borrowdale Show.

Stanley Jackson sorting ewes and lambs in the pens at The Nook, Rosthwaite. The farm is about 500 acres with some common fell. At lambing time, Stanley brings all his ewes into the pastures around the farm, on the flat fields between the Derwent and the Stonethwaite Beck.

TWO

Fit for the Fell

Farmers are not as dour or as taciturn as they sometimes seem. Holding a conversation is usually a matter of measured phrases and silences, punctuated by subtle inflections of breath. I made the mistake once of arriving at West Head Farm, at the head of Thirlmere, and suggesting to David Bland that I could chat to him about the farm while we walked out, with his sons Peter and Gavin, to check a cut of sheep on the slopes of Steel Fell.

Anyone familiar with the road from Keswick to Grasmere will know Steel Fell, a beautiful but steep little hill to the north-west of Dunmail Raise. David's farm extends to 4000 acres, embracing the west face of Helvellyn. Every slope is acute: I knew I was going to be in trouble. The first half was manageable, the third quarter was difficult, and the last was a blur. The gaps in our conversation served a dual purpose: for David to check his sheep and for me to gasp for breath. Meanwhile his sons (one a rugby player, the other a champion fell-runner) had disappeared over the crest and were already boulder-hopping their way home. David waited for me. Nothing was said about my embarrassing lack of stamina, but I think David had taken my measure.

This had been at the back end. In the following spring, much recovered, I called at West Head again, to see the lambing. Fortunately this is all done close to the farm: I would not have dared to suggest another walk. David Bland's Herdwick sheep are tough. Given the choice they would spend all their time on the high fells, in all weathers. They are also very conservative; in the winter they will not touch silage or turnips. However, in April the ewes are brought down to the intakes, where there is more shelter and the grass is better. Thus they can still

fend for themselves without being fussed over. Each morning, David checks them, and if any are in trouble he helps.

It was a beautiful day. A willow warbler was singing from somewhere in the birches by the road. Further up the valley, the air over Dunmail Raise was sharp and clear. Below us there was a sudden whoosh as a flight of pigeons dashed north, very low to avoid the local peregrines. Sheep covered the intakes. At this time, 1995, there were about three thousand sheep on the farm (it had been four thousand before the introduction of the ESA Scheme, and it was destined to be still less again after the start of Enhancement Schemes). Most seemed to be Herdwicks: the ewes have a pale grey fleece, while the hoggs or young females are chocolate brown, and the lambs are sooty black. The effect here, on a scree-covered pasture, was like a shifting tweed quilt.

It took about an hour to cover the lambing fields. One ewe needed attention because it was having trouble giving birth to a large-headed lamb. Another had already had its single lamb but had taken against it and was not allowing it to suckle. The on-the-spot solution was to hold her firmly and let the lamb suckle for a few minutes, to get her used to the idea. It worked, at least for as long as we were nearby. Finally there was a ewe with twins. On lowland farms this would be a normal and efficient state of affairs, but on a hill farm the grazing is too poor for any ewe to feed two lambs. Under such circumstances one of them has to be taken away and 'set on' to another ewe that has lost its own lamb. So we carried one black lamb back to the farm, then had a cup of tea and watched as Peter skinned a dead lamb from the previous evening and fitted the gory coat over the new lamb to be fostered.

By the end of the morning all was well at West Head and everyone was relaxed and chatty in the sunshine. Later, as I drove north and east, over Hartside Pass, I realised Geltdale had vanished in a grey shroud, and before I had reached Alston there was a squall of spindrift and snow. It would not, after all, be an easy lambing.

Above and opposite: *Hardy sheep like the Herdwick are best left to lamb on their own. In this sequence of pictures, taken at Rosthwaite, the birth is straightforward and the only trouble the ewe has is getting the lamb onto its feet. Herdwick lambs are always black, but they usually have white ear-tips and a few silvery hairs on their back.*

David Bland of West Head, setting out to look the sheep on the lower slopes of Steel Fell. Down below is the pass of Dunmail Raise. David's farm runs to 4000 acres and in the 1980s he would have run four thousand sheep on it. By the mid-1990s he had cut down the stock by over a quarter as part of an ESA scheme. The payments were a big help, but at the same time his landlord (NW Water) had just tripled his rent.

'Herdwicks don't like fuss. They have an independent streak and are likely to leave their
lamb if you bother them.' But sometimes a ewe takes against its lamb anyway, and has to
be re-introduced to it. David Bland of West Head, near Thirlmere.

Herdwicks can look like teddy-bears, but they sometimes turn nasty. This one had been kicking its lamb and not letting it feed. David Bland is holding the ewe so that the lamb can suckle. Once this has happened there is a good chance she will accept it again.

Peter Bland setting on a lamb at West Head Farm. If fell sheep have twins they are only allowed to keep one of them (there is not enough food value in the vegetation for her to feed two successfully). A lamb is set on to a foster-mother by covering it with the skin of the mother's own dead lamb. For a while she might not accept the replacement, which is why Peter has tethered her in a kennel and is helping the lamb to suckle. Its white ear-tips stand out in the shadows.

Summer at Loughrigg: good weather and a time of easy living for ewes and lambs.

Opposite: *A damp dreary day in October. Donald Hodgson of Town Head (foreman at Kirkstone Quarry for four days a week: farmer for the other three) is bringing in a Swaledale ('Swaddle') lamb 'done badly' by the ticks in the bracken country.*

The long walk down Greenburn Bottom, with the slopes of Helm Crag on the right.
Donald Hodgson of Town Head.

Tea and biscuits in the yard at Town Head near Grasmere. Donald Hodgson with the teapot: Gavin, Peter and David Bland, and Robert Dixon, have just helped bring in the ewes and lambs from Steel Fell. Good neighbours are a blessing for any farmer.

Swaledale sheep on the north cliff-top of High Cup Nick, the most dramatic landscape feature in the Pennines. The amphitheatre of grey dolerite faces the Eden Valley.

THREE

The Golden Fleece

When we have all sheared our jolly jolly sheep
What joy could be greater than to talk of their increase?

We'll pipe and we'll sing, we'll dance in a ring
When each lad takes his lass all on the green grass
And it's oh! to plough where the fat oxen graze low
And the lads and the lasses do sheep-shearing go.

I have never seen anyone clipping sheep with the sort of ecstatic joy suggested in traditional folk songs. I think this is probably because most songs about country life were written by Victorian vicars who had never experienced it. But perhaps the songs were meant to be sung after the work was over and everyone had gathered for a boozy annual celebration in the farmer's barn.

In southern England the farm labourers' get-together came after the harvest (as in *Far from the Madding Crowd*), but in the north it was usually after clipping day. Each hill farm could call on a gang of friends and neighbours to help, to gather and to clip. In the 1990s I knew of just two farms where this still happened, and for one day at least the farmyard was noisy with children's laughter as friends and relations came together to share a seasonal labour. Most hill farms now support one family; the rural economy has moved on and friends and relations have been cast to the winds, to make a better living elsewhere.

Wool created wealth and prestige for medieval Britain, lining the pockets of monks and bishops. For centuries the woolsack was a symbol of national prosperity: packhorse trails criss-crossed the Pennine moors and carried the harvest of a million fleeces south to service weavers and millers, as the Industrial Revolution gathered pace.

When I was a boy, we pushed a set of pram wheels around the streets collecting old woollens, to sell to a local rag merchant. Moth-eaten pullovers and worn-out blankets earned far more money than a paper-round did. Now in a post-industrial society, there is no market for wool, especially the coarse sort produced by hill breeds. And while it is tempting to regret the change I can also remember, in the 1950s, having to wear a 'winter vest', which itched horribly, and put on darned socks which were always uncomfortable and made our feet sore. Wool had its down side; I have no nostalgic yearnings for those vests and socks. A few years ago I visited a weaver on Harris and bought from her a pair of 'crottle socks' – made from local Blackface wool and dyed with lichens. I used them as wellie-socks and they lasted about a month: not a good investment. Was I encouraging a traditional cottage industry, a cultural treasure and a contribution to the Hebridean economy? Or just wasting my money?

Contract shearers of a dozen nationalities, working their way from the Falklands to Norway, arrive in Cumbria each summer and spend late June and early July on the hill farms. Many smaller farms make do on their own, with sons and daughters taking on the clipping, but it is very hard physical work and is one of the few times when a farmer is usually content to pay for outside labour. The cost works out (at 2004 prices) at about 60p per sheep. At one time an average hill farm, stocked with Swaledales or Herdwicks, would receive an annual wool cheque of about £2500 – enough to cover all costs and leave something to put towards a new TV and a couple of tups. Now it is about £400, and some farmers have taken to burning the fleeces rather than sending them to the wool warehouse. When I was visiting Birkdale Farm, a singularly remote little place below High Cup, I was told that over the decades they had always buried any useless fleeces in the field next to the yard, and it now provided the only well-drained standing around the farm: a sort of deep-pile carpet. Any new barn extension at Birkdale is going to need firm foundations. The farm has never hired any shearers, but neither has it ever made enough money to pay for them.

In 1994 I spent a morning at a wool warehouse at Hexham, following a load of Swaledale fleeces in from Garrigill and hoping to see them processed (Herdwick fleeces went to Carnforth: the rest to Bradford, Galashiels or Hexham). But there was a backlog of several months; only fine fleeces (like Texels) were dealt with straight away. The rest waited their turn. Over thirty thousand sheets (ie bags, or sacks) were collected in a year, from over three thousand farms. Each sheet contained eighty to a hundred Swaledale fleeces.

I watched some being graded: each sheet was emptied onto a table and the fleeces stretched upside down and held out with skewers, then released so they still held together, to be vacuum packed and dispatched. The grading depended on quality and was mainly determined by breed. Length and fineness were important: the amount of cotting, grey fibre and kemp, discolour and dip colour (anything from Venetian red to engine-oil) all counted against a fleece. Farmers received their payments in two instalments, the first on account, the second after weighing and grading. Bearing in mind what I had seen bagged up on Pennine and Lakeland farms, I did not think many of the farmers I knew would be buying new TVs this year.

Most of the wool produced in Britain today goes for carpet-making. It remains a mystery to me why carpets are so expensive when the raw material is now so cheap. On a recent visit to the new offices of the National Trust's Borrowdale team I was greatly taken by their floor-coverings: natural Herdwick carpeting, very attractive. When I contacted the supplier in Kendal, I was quoted a price so out of my price-range that I blinked and knew what it must be like for sturgeon-fishermen to walk into a reception at the Ritz.

I called in one last time in early July to see a clipping day in the Lake District. Leslie Kyle of Sykes Farm was shearing tups and was proud of them. One in particular looked impressive – a good head but the fleece paler than usual (so he had bought it for £150 rather than £400: everyone likes to show off a bargain). Against the shed wall there were rolled fleeces of a hundred different hues, all Herdwicks and beautiful. After the shearing, and after seeing the cattle in for milking, I took Leslie for a drink across the road to the Fish Hotel in Buttermere. For the first few minutes he was smiling and talkative, but gradually he fell silent and I realised he was bone-weary: simply exhausted:

...Lambs to rear and sheep to shear.
Health and contentment the countrymen wear.

Bringing in stray Swaledales for clipping, down the valley of the Maize Beck from High Cup to Birkdale Farm.

An unusually dry and sunny afternoon after a long drive, with time for Brian Bainbridge to take things easy as his dog pushes the sheep over Grain Beck to Birkdale Farm.

Through the gate and off the fell: Brian Bainbridge driving a cut of Swaledales into the field of Birkdale Farm. The farm includes 3000 acres of fell, but only a 150 acres of inbye pasture. The plastic bag in Brian's pocket contains a bottle of whisky, a present from his neighbours on the Dufton side of the fell for gathering and sorting their strays.

Clipping in the byre at Birkdale Farm: Raymond Hutchinson, Lee Stevenson, Andrew Bousfield and Heather Kindleyside.

Mike Kyle hand-clipping a young Herdwick on a traditional trestle, at Sykes Farm in Buttermere.

When sheep are clipped they usually give in gracefully and suffer the indignity with snooty indifference. In this case, the sheep (a North Country Cheviot tup) is so big that Leslie Kyle is finding it difficult to support its weight while he works.

Leslie Kyle clipping a Herdwick tup in the barn at Sykes Farm. The sheep is taking a polite interest in what is going on around it.

Shades of grey: Herdwick fleeces rolled and ready to go into the sack.

FOUR

Wasdale Gather

According to Housman, writing in 1800, everything in Wasdale 'is rural, and every scene in the true style of pastoral beauty and simplicity'. I have never had much truck with romantic poets (Wordsworth included), who had little real knowledge of the places they are describing. However, you would be hard-pressed to find a prettier place than Wasdale on a sunny day. The unspoilt nature of the valley is partly due to its isolation, emphasised by the contrast between the verdant wooded slopes and fields at its foot and the austere mountain range at its head. Between the extremes is the deepest lake in England (Wastwater) and the highest and most desolate of screes in Europe.

I knew the valley well. Like thousands of walkers, I had used the car-park and camp-site at Wasdale Head to explore the high western fells and take the stony tracks up to Scafell and Great Gable. But I had also been impressed by the ancient field systems and clearance cairns, and by the scatter of sheep that adds a sense of proportion to the mighty landscape. After having followed several drives or gathers on the lower fells, I knew it would be hard to come away with any worthwhile shepherding pictures from the mountains. But I had to try.

I did not know any of the Wasdale farmers, least of all the few who worked the high fells. In the end I tried to contact Nigel Sale at the National Trust, their Public Relations Manager with whom I had worked to produce a series of leaflets about the Lakeland valleys. On the morning I phoned, Nigel was out and they put me through to someone else who 'handles the media'. I explained I was a lone photographer wanting to take pictures in Wasdale and needing a contact number for one of their farms. Not a problem, was the reply: the fee would be £1000, or perhaps £2000. I politely declined, and waited until the afternoon when Nigel was back in the office. Clearly, the Trust is justified in charging a fee for film companies and fashion shoots on its land, but I did not see how this could apply to me: I was certainly not making any money out of the project. Fortunately, Nigel agreed and he put me in touch with Scott Naylor, the tenant farmer at Row Head.

Wasdale is to the south-west of the high fells at the core of the Lake District. To get there from the east you have to drive a long arc to the north or south, or cut across the middle via the spectacular passes of Wrynose and Hardknott. Except in icy weather I always took the passes, to be down into Eskdale before the tourist traffic started. Via leafy Miterdale and Santon Bridge, then Nether Wasdale, the last approach to Row Head at the very top of the valley was all shattered screes and indigo water: a big landscape of brutal simplicity. Then you were into a tiny patch of green meadows and drystone walls, tucked below the towering slopes of Yewbarrow, Kirk Fell, Lingmell and Sca Fell.

The first time I called at Row Head I had expected bad weather and a cautious welcome. I was wrong about the weather – it was a glorious sunny day – but the Naylors were a taciturn family: they hardly spoke even to each other and were guarded about having me following them around. However, Scott made it clear I was to be tolerated, and his word was law. Row Head runs three stocks of sheep, on Lingmell, Yewbarrow and Mosedale. Altogether, there are four gathers a year (lambing, clipping, spaining and tipping), each requiring ten days' work. There was little time for chatter.

I followed Heather and Mike Naylor onto the precipitous east slope of Yewbarrow and left them to work their dogs over the summit ridge. Alan and Paul were away on the other side, circling around to the west. The climb was gruelling, especially on a warm morning. Just below the rocky collar around the summit I stopped and sat among bushes of bilberry and picked handfuls of big ripe berries to quench my thirst. The air was sharp and clear, and the view both south over Wastwater and east over the dale-head, to the Sca Fell massif, was of arresting beauty. There was no point in trying to chase the flurries of sheep as dogs rounded them into the saddle between the summit cairns: the gather in its early stages is all about the dogs, often working out of sight as they hussle ewes and lambs and push them along narrow ledges and through bracken beds. After about ten minutes of silence there was a burst of action as a handful of sheep crashed past me, through the bilberry and onto a rock ledge. For a moment they looked for a way down, but then turned back and melted into the undergrowth. There was a minute's stillness and then one of the dogs appeared and vanished. Then there was nothing and all the action had shifted down to the lower slopes. Ones and twos of sheep had become twenties and thirties. I followed Heather, with her dogs Meg and Blue, down between boulders towards the intakes. Suddenly we were in a drift of two or three hundred sheep, all fast on the move, heading north-east to a gate above Lingmell Beck. Once through the gate, it was a short run to cross the little bridge to the pens. And then it was all over and everyone was back at the farm for dinner.

The images of the cut of sheep driving towards Lingmell had made the day worthwhile, but it had all been over too quickly. I talked to Scott Naylor and learned that another gather was due in a couple of days, this time north to Mosedale. I drove home via the hair-pins of Hardknott, still in diamond-bright sunshine, looking forward to another breathless day among the Herdwicks.

Of course, it did not work out quite as I had expected. As I climbed out of Little Langdale two mornings later, in the middle of July, Wrynose was in thick mist and Eskdale was awash. The cloud-base was less than 1000 feet. By the time I reached Row Head I had convinced myself that my journey from the east was all a waste of time. Scott was monosyllabic and the family was bickering. We all sat in the darkened farmhouse parlour for an hour, waiting. Eventually, Scott took a last look outside, and without any sign that I could see, the decision was taken and we were off.

I can remember little about the long walk up Mosedale and Black Sail Pass. Pillar and Red Pike should have been ahead and to the left of us, but we saw nothing in the driving rain. Everyone was in shirtsleeves except me: I could not see how it could ever turn sunny again. On the north shoulder of Kirk Fell we stopped and Mike and Alan talked through their strategy, with sweeping motions of their hands denoting either how the mist was clearing or how the sheep (which had been invisible so far) would be drawn around the Ennerdale basin. Away to the east, across the River Liza, we could see the shepherds of Seathwaite driving a cut of Herdwicks the other way, over Gillercomb Head or around Grey Knotts into Borrowdale.

After a while our own gather began: Heather and Alan worked to the west, into the head of Ennerdale Forest and up the slope, while Paul took the high fell and worked down: where they met they turned south and pushed the sheep up the steep slope and over the saddle into Mosedale. At some point, missed in the excitement, the rain stopped and there were shreds and patches of blue sky overhead. Things started to go well and everyone relaxed. I had followed Paul on his sweep of the high fell. When he suddenly stopped and knelt down to drink at a stream, then lit a cigarette and called his dogs in, I knew that we were heading for home.

It was 3.00 pm before we were back in Row Head farmhouse. Over a mug of tea I took out my sodden notebook and tried to read it. It made little sense, but that hardly mattered:

Heaped up around Pyat How (did I mean Boat How?), then contoured and over side-beck, then up Black Sail. Paul working three dogs: Speck, Glen, Fly. Calling all the time, just the name –

'Fly, Fly, Fly, Fly, Fly…', pointing left or right with his crook, keeping eye contact with them.

When I left the farm at about 4.00pm, I noticed Heather in the pens, separating out the strays and getting things ready for clipping the next morning. Scott had been right about the weather after all.

Gathering sheep on the east slope of Yewbarrow, at Wasdale Head. Mike Naylor of Row Head is working his dogs to the far left of the picture, where a group of Herdwick ewes and lambs is disappearing over the rise, down towards Mosedale. The mountains at the head of the valley are Kirk Fell and Great Gable, with the slope of Lingmell on the right. The crazy paving pattern of Wasdale Head's walls is an indication of their antiquity. Most of them are 6 feet thick and 6 feet high: they were created as much to clear stones away as to separate individual fields.

Heather Naylor working sheep down the steep slope of Yewbarrow.

Off the fell and through the gate at the foot of Yewbarrow, near Down-in-the-Dale Bridge.

The Yewbarrow heaft of three hundred ewes and lambs, moving north above the Mosedale Beck, with Wasdale Head Hotel and Kirk Fell in the distance.

When sheep have not had to go very far they travel at a surprising speed. Even this late in a gather, half a mile from home, something can go wrong and they can veer off and double back.

Herdwick sheep, still running, crossing the packhorse bridge over Mosedale Beck into the pens at Row Head. The ewes are ready for shearing, but first their levels of radio-activity will be monitored (there were still post-Chenobyl restrictions in place when these pictures were taken).

Shepherds and dogs follow the sheep home. Alan and Mike Naylor, their cousin Paul, father Scott and sister Heather. The gather had taken about five hours and everyone is ready for their dinner (meat pie, jelly and tinned peaches).

Pages 54–60: *The Mosedale gather, from Row Head Farm. The day had started wet and misty. At the back of Kirk Fell there was a long conversation between Mike and Alan Naylor before they sent the dogs round in a wide arc towards the head of Ennerdale. The drive back ran perfectly: the fell-tops cleared and there were patches of blue sky to finish the day.*

Down the track and across Fogmire Beck, a field away from Row Head at the end of the Mosedale gather.

Milking in the converted byre at Sykes Farm.

FIVE

Cattle Drives

I remember my Great Uncle Jack with all the clarity and confusion of a town-boy let loose on the land, learning where milk came from and having it squirted at me straight from the udder.

I would give anything now to be back on holiday at Leashaw Farm in the late 1950s, with the cobbles of the stockyard hard and hot and dusty against my toes on an evening after haymaking: with the Dairy Shorthorns on their way down the track over the canal bridge to the byre, and Uncle Jack slapping their haunches and shouting at us to get a bucket and go and collect the eggs from the chickens in the hay-loft: with the sickly-sweetness of cattle and hay filling the air, and the vermillion of the evening sky soaking the stonework of the farmhouse, turning it peach and rose: to be scared of everything, of Uncle Jack because he was deaf and shouted everything, even his whispers: of 'China' the goose who scratched around the midden and always chased us: of not being able to do anything properly: of having to go to bed early and leave it all behind so we could be back at school on Monday. And one day we did leave it behind, and we never went back.

Mixed family farms, too small to pay their way, have been dispatched to oblivion. I would certainly not want to try to make ends meet now in dairy farming with anything less than two hundred cows and two converted stables, let to the sort of people who can afford folk-memories of the golden days. Leashaw Farm was never more than a subsistence enterprise. My mother stopped us going there because we always came back with fleas, caught off the farmyard cats.

Mike Kyle walking his herd of Ayrshire cattle through Buttermere and on to their milking parlour at Sykes Farm.

Cumbria yields more milk than any other county in England. The Solway Plain through Carlisle to the Eden is first class cow country, mainly herds of Holsteins with a few Ayrshires and Jerseys. Foot and mouth disease in 2001 wreaked havoc but led to a shake-out among dairy farmers – many took the opportunity to retire, or stayed in their homes but leased out the land. Amalgamation has made sense all round: there are more farmers' sons in accountancy than there are in farming, and there is no pressure these days to pass on a tenancy or to leave behind a legacy on the hoof. All of this has resulted in a more effective and efficient farming industry.

Finding small-scale dairy units on family farms was a lot easier in the 1990s. Since my main concern with this project was the closeness of the relationship between people and the land, I was not attracted to silage pits, feeder wagons and robot units. My most enjoyable day at milking was at Buttermere with John Kyle – an engaging curmudgeon who sometimes wore clogs around the farmyard but was just as likely to be wearing new Scarpa boots in the slurry. He held trenchant views on every subject and laid the blame for the woes of the present country-side squarely on bad farming, including his own. 'If only I'd known better when I was younger!' he said. 'I'd have looked after my meadows if I'd known about the herbs.' He remembers having to take his wife down to the lake-shore to identify a flower he did not recognise, only to be told that it was a cowslip. Now he has cowslip seedlings in the stockyard, with wire baskets over the top to keep the sheep off.

I went down to the shore of Crummock Water with John to bring in his herd of Ayrshires one morning in early July. They were not of text-book physique nor deportment (John liked them small and dark-mottled), but they looked perfect in the Lakeland setting. They came up the lane from the lake at a snail's pace, stopping to browse on ash leaves as they passed the back of the Fish Hotel: a barman appeared waving a tea-towel to chase them away, but they ignored him. Once all seventeen cows were into the byre, the milking took an hour. Each animal was held by a wooden-toggled rope and the unit moved from stall to stall down the vacuum line. Then John's son Leslie drove them out of the yard again and along the road to High House, where there was good but steep pasture. A time-consuming and inefficient twice-a-day business that has no place in modern farming, unless like the Kyles you are heafted to the land.

Dairy cattle are usually put to a beef bulls to produce crosses for suckler calves: the staple livestock of upland pastures. Whether the present system will endure much longer is open to question. Many farmers believe that their land has been well served by maintaining a 'balanced ticket' – running both sheep and cattle, because the animals graze in different ways and thereby keep the sward healthy. But some cheerful souls see no future for cattle at all.

Virtually all cattle in upland Britain today are inwintered, spending five or six months of the year in sheds, where they are fed on silage and concentrates. They see the light of day in April, ready for the spring bite. Fifty years ago, old Cumberland was full of Hereford x Dairy Shorthorns, then Hereford x Friesians. From the 1970s there has been a near-complete change, and most suckler calves, fattened for the big autumn sales, are Limousin x Holstein. The old dairy breeds like Ayrshire and British Friesian had a dual purpose function: a respectable milk yield with butterfat, and good conformation with a solid rump. The same cannot be said of the Holstein – a specialist milk-volume producer with a scrawny back-end and 'coat-hanger' hips. But the conformation hardly matters now: the important thing is that they grow quickly. 'Continental' breeds (Charolais, Simmental, Limousin, Belgian Blue) are hefty but delicate – they shiver in cold weather and sometimes get irritable. One stockman I spoke to summed up his 'Limmie crosses' as 'top of the list for turning rubbish into meat, but they're crackers; not right in the head.'

Driving inwintered cattle out to pasture is not like driving cows to the milking parlour. If they have spent months in confinement they are inclined to appreciate their freedom for a few days and behave like children let out of school. When Jim Akrigg of Westwood Farm told me they would soon be moving a herd of Angus x Friesians up to their Woodside pastures I had no great expectations of good photographs: I knew there would be a catch.

The Askrigg family had come to Westwood in 1946, when it was a little dairy farm. They had spent several decades building it up by acquiring extra stints and allotments, and by fencing the fells and establishing a heaft of sheep and a suckler herd. But building it up piecemeal had created a few problems. The cattle from the sheds had only a few days of grass before they had to be moved to high fell pasture, a couple of miles away on the other side of Brough. The tradition was to have them ready at dawn and then drive them through the town before they got in the way of the traffic.

In the event it was like a stampede in a John Ford movie, with Jim Askrigg's son riding a motor-bike rather than a chestnut mare. A hundred Angus x Friesians thundered through the town leaving copious trails of slurry in the bus lane. I expected them to slow down when the open road climbed steeply to the east, but they kept going. My pictures were all taken on the run. Eventually the herd was headed off left, through a gate and down a dusty hairpin track. The last I saw of them they were still heading for the far horizon and the open range.

Of all the comings and goings of farmers since I photographed them for *True to the Land*, the emigration of the Askriggs to Canada is the least surprising.

Back to the pasture at High House, above Buttermere in the Lake District. Leslie Kyle holding the gate for the milking herd of Ayrshires.

Once one of the most popular breeds of cattle for milking and dual-purpose, the Ayrshire is now a rare sight in Cumbria.

The grass on the other side of a fence always tastes better. A Friesian cow in the Naddle Valley.

Friesians at Fellside Farm, near Caldbeck ('Back o' Skiddaw'). They look very solid and chunky compared with the Holsteins we are now used to seeing.

Holstein calves on buttercup-covered pastures near Carlisle. This is the breed of the moment and probably constitutes 95 per cent of the county's dairy herd.

Some of the best dairy country in Britain: Holsteins on the merse of the Solway shore.

Joseph and John Hewson with one of their Dairy Shorthorn bulls at Parton Farm near Wigton. 'We've kept Herefords and Shorthorns for thirty years, but they've gone out of fashion,' said John, wistfully. A few weeks before this picture was taken John had been over to Limerick for a weekend to judge Shorthorns. It was the first time he had been abroad ('except for the Isle of Man').

Dairy Shorthorns coming into the sheds at Parton Farm, Wigton.

The annual drive of Jim Askrigg's suckler herd, through the streets of Brough in early June to get them onto the fell pasture to the north of the village. Jim's farm is unusually spread out: 'Everything's 4 miles away. It can be a bit of a headache.'

The long climb to Woodside.

Down the track on the last leg of the cattle-drive. Why Jim liked to keep one white beast in the herd is a mystery. He also kept a Vietnamese pot-bellied pig as a pet.

Jim Askrigg counting his cattle onto the fell near Brough, in south-east Cumbria. Ninety-four in all: 'Angus x Friesian, run with a Limmy bull.'

Traditional hay-meadow near Alston: a tapestry of red clover, pignut, common sorrel, yellow rattle and meadow buttercup. The grasses include cocksfoot, crested dogstail and soft brome. It will have taken decades or even centuries to establish this composition: the hay will be cut in a few days, after the herbs have gone to seed.

SIX

Hay and Hard Times

Working with nature has its ups and downs. There can be few more rewarding moments for a farmer than seeing a barn-full of dry hay stacked and away, and few more depressing moments than having the skies open over a field of cut grass. Two or three days of sun are all a farmer asks, but it is often denied.

Haymaking must have been one of the defining discoveries of prehistory. To raise stock in one place and be able to feed them through the year, rather than to herd animals from one wild pasture to another, meant that it was possible for families to establish farmsteads and fields, and permanent homes. Stability was as important to Stone Age farmers as it is to post-industrial agri-barons. The amount of hay that a farm could grow dictated how many sheep and cattle could be maintained through the winter. Through the Bronze Age, the climate of Northern England was as good as it has ever been, but in the Iron Age it deteriorated again and there was an unsettled period as crops failed and ranching took over from mixed farming. Extended family groups, under powerful 'chieftains', took to rustling across an open landscape. It must have been like the Wild West, with homesteaders turned off their land by cattle-barons.

In Cumbria this state of affairs must have lasted well into historic times (though the Romans would not have allowed armed gangs to wander around the countryside). When British and Viking settlers arrived to farm the uplands they were not the first to do so. When they built stone walls around the valley-sides and grew hay to over-winter their stock, they were simply adopting a pattern of agriculture that had

been successful before. And for another fifteen centuries, until the 1960s, the system would endure.

People of a certain age treasure memories of flowery meadows. Old farm-workers share the memory and the nostalgia, but unlike the rest of their generation they know why and when all the flowers disappeared. In post-war Britain, fields of grass were grazed through the winter and then left to grow a crop of hay. The manure, scattered over several months, was an effective fertiliser: by June or early July the meadows were rich in flowers like eyebright, yellow rattle and sorrel. The hay was cut after the herbs had seeded, when the grass was at its most nutritious. With the introduction of artificial fertilisers, grasses could be treated with extra nitrogen to make them grow thicker and juicier. But the grasses then swamped out the herbs. Then silage-making was introduced, in which the grass crop can be cut earlier and clamped or bagged damp, then left to ferment. This meant even bigger yields, but the cut was taken before the herbs had flowered, so they could set no seed. The result over most of the country today is bright green fields, rows of black silage bags, and a lot of old people with flowery memories.

I do not believe for a moment that living at the foot of Shap, Wild Boar Fell or Lingmoor would have been an easy life when hay was the essential crop of the high valleys. On the contrary, I think it could have been a heart-breaking endurance. If you look closely at a fireplace in one of the quaint cottages dotted around the Lake District you will find a place in the chimney where cuts of mutton were smoked. 'Collops' or strips of greasy mutton were the only meat available for most people in the winter. Each little farm could sustain only the animals it could feed in the worst weather. Because the amount of valley meadows was limited, hay was in short supply and only used for next season's breeding stock. The remaining cattle were sent to market, and the sheep were either sold or smoked. Farming would have been hand-to-mouth and grindingly poor, as well as unhealthy. The fact that the countryside was prettier would have been lost on the locals.

Every now and then, while travelling through Cumbria and especially in the east, I have seen fields of hay among the silage, as if someone has deliberately taken the risk and hoped for the sun. Hay provides a much better balanced diet than silage, at least according to farmers I have spoken to in the Pennines. Near Alston I met one family raking the corners of their home meadow, gleaning the last bale of hay. They had plenty of silage already bagged from the banks of the Eden. According to the farmer, his sheep would eat silage, but they didn't like it. He kept his hay for his best tups and show animals, to pamper them through the winter. The special ingredient, he said, was the flavour of the herbs. 'Just smell that,' he said, thrusting a handful of dry stems under my nose. 'Vernal and clover. Lovely!'

Over the years, people have discovered ways of augmenting their hay. Cumbria is a landscape of pastures and meadows, walls and trees. On the fells of old Westmorland the valley fields have always been walled rather than hedged, but as most walkers will know, there are always trees nearby. Oaks, growing naturally, were left to stand on grassy knolls in the pastures, to provide shade. But oak leaves are full of tannins and unpalatable to stock. Along the walls, ash trees were lopped or pollarded so that they could provide a crop of useful poles every few years, to be used for tool handles and fencing. Meanwhile, the foliage could be cut for the sheep, who found it good to eat and a change from their usual fell diet. So anything grown on Lakeland farms had a use or could be eaten. The Lake District's ash pollards are now given special status because of their antiquity and because their hollow trunks have become miniature wildlife reserves – places for bats and barn owls to roost in an otherwise hostile countryside.

I visited a couple of farms in the Lake District to see their ash pollards lopped. The work is carried out every fifteen to twenty years. If it were not done regularly the trees would eventually die. Pollarding extends the life of trees almost to infinity, though they become objects of distorted gothic beauty in the process.

At one farm in Borrowdale, the National Trust tenant refused to do the job himself, because a venerable pollard had died on him a few years before and he had taken it personally. Instead, a Trust estate-worker brought in his chain-saw and the job was over in a trice, with the poles carted out of the field. This was not really what I had expected and I was relieved at the second farm, in Little Langdale, where George Birkitt let me see how it should be done 'properly'. By this he meant with a bill-hook while balancing on the crown of the tree boll. It looked precarious, but the end result was satisfactory. When he shushed in a few of his tups from High Birk How they immediately demonstrated the hidden attraction of ash trees by nibbling off the bark. According to George the best way with ash was to leave the cut poles in the fields after pollarding, so that the sheep could take advantage of the nutritious outer layer before the poles were taken away to be sliced up for firewood. At the end of the day, I was unsure whether it was the bark or the foliage that had been eaten by sheep in the old, hard days, but I now know for a fact that Herdwick tups have teeth like chisels.

A modern grass mix based on rye-grass and clover, perfect for a high hay yield on a short term ley: the field will be dug up and reseeded (or replanted with a cereal crop) after a few years.

Muck-spreading – the best way to feed a meadow because the nutrients are released slowly, allowing herbs to flourish as well as grasses. John Dodd of Sillywrea Farm.

Cutting hay on a damp meadow north of Alston.

Cutting hay the quiet way (but it also takes a lot longer!). John Dodd of Sillywrea Farm near Langley, with Monty and Jock.

Loading hay-bales on a summer's evening at Sillywrea Farm. David Wise and Scottie.

A Pennine meadow, on a hazy June day. Looking across the South Tyne Valley, near Garrigill, with Cross Fell on the horizon.

The same meadow in July, and the last patch of grass being cut.

Above and opposite: *Baling and loading hay near Garrigill: the same meadow as on previous pages.*

Midwinter, over the snow-covered meadow to Cross Fell. Again the same meadow as on pages 86–89.

A patchwork of hayfields, and the crop nearly in. Martindale in the Lake District. The best fields in the valley are enclosed within an ancient stone wall: beyond this on the slopes are more recently established intakes of pasture, once used to graze cattle. Sheep would have spent most of their time on the fell, but 'ingangs' or walled droveways would have allowed shepherds to drive them to the farm for lambing and clipping.

Ash pollards in field walls near Grasmere. Ash leaves are palatable to cattle and sheep, and the foliage would once have been gathered to augment their diet. These Friesians would enjoy a taste, given the chance.

George Birkett of High Birk How in Little Langdale, cutting ash poles from an old pollard. Afterwards the trees look silly for two or three years, but the process increases their life-span and is a traditional source of 'small-wood', for hand-tools, fencing etc. George was going to let these poles lie for a while, to feed his tups, then cut up logs for firewood.

Cutting ash poles: a precarious business.

George Birkett driving his tups into the inbye fields, where two trees had been pollarded.

Herdwick tups nibbling the bark off ash poles at High Birk How. Early winter in Little Langdale: Lingmoor Fell on the skyline.

Borrowdale panorama from Yew Crag. For centuries the working landscape comprised flat valley meadows and arable fields, 'intakes' of grazing pastures, oakwoods, and high fells for sheep. Today we still enjoy the landscape, but have no use for its products.

SEVEN

Work in the Woods

Losing yourself is a lot easier in a wood than it is anywhere else. When people walk on fell-tops they want to experience a sense of solitude and freedom, but they also want to know exactly where they are. This is not always possible among trees. The first time I steered a path alone through the New Forest, trying to get from Beaulieu Road to Brockenhurst, I emerged within a hundred yards of where I had started from. The same happened when I explored a 'secret' location near Carlisle, where a colony of marsh fritillary butterflies still survives in a clearing in the middle of a broadleaf plantation. I completed a narrow circle around the clearing without ever seeing it, let alone a butterfly. Trees have a way of pointing you in the wrong direction and making you feel foolish.

It is a tempting cliché to say that two or three centuries ago, Britain was a heavily-wooded country, where a squirrel could skip from branch to branch and travel thus from coast to coast. This may have been the case in prehistory, but by medieval times most of the lowlands had been cleared for agriculture: the remaining 'wildwood' was set aside within obvious boundaries, for hunting and to provide fuel, pannage and crops of timber. The main systems of woodland management were 'wood pasture' – growing mature trees and grazing domestic animals on the ground layer of vegetation – and 'coppice-with-standards' – interspersing the big timber trees with productive short-rotation crops of 'smallwood', often hazel.

Once the stems of a coppice stool have been cut down to the ground they immediately start to grow again, taking ten or fifteen years to get back to their original height. In its productive heyday, perhaps in the eighteenth century, a wood could be separated into twenty or thirty blocks or 'coops' and harvested in a continuous rotation, the coppice leased by the estate to woodmen and the timber trees cut every two or three generations to pay off taxes and death duties. This system of management was so taken for granted that when coppicing became uneconomic, by the early years of the twentieth century at the latest, nobody noticed until flowers and butterflies had disappeared too: opening the canopy every few years had also encouraged sun-loving wildlife.

In the 1970s I visited several southern woods where coppicing was still carried out and I thought they were magical places. When I moved to the North in 1980 it took me a couple of years to discover that although the ecology was different, the general idea of exploiting woodland had been the same, as had been the fate of the coppices. What at first looked like quilts of brushwood on steep valley-sides turned out to be grown-out groves of wych-elm and alder: impenetrable and very easy to get lost in.

Coppicing hazel in Long Itchington Wood, Warwickshire.

Cutting thatching spars, Cranbourne Chase.

I found the Cumbrian oakwoods almost by accident. Like most people I was getting to know the Lake District by heading uphill seeking the highest ground. In Borrowdale this meant parking in one of the little villages like Rosthwaite or Grange and climbing the steep rocky paths towards Dale Head, Ullscarf and Glaramara. In between the intake fields and the open fells there were hanging woods of grey, gnarled oaks. Not like the high forest of the South, with wide canopies of tall maiden trees and an understorey of holly or hazel, but packs of stocky sessile oaks, crouched against westerly gales and cold rain.

I explored them one by one: Johnny Wood, Stonethwaite and Seatoller Woods, Castle Crag and Great Wood. The common factor was that they had all been intensively managed until the eighteenth century. In some places a little further afield, from Windermere and Coniston south to Morecambe Bay, there were left-overs of woodland industries into the twentieth century. It was a surprise to talk to local woodmen like David Tomasson and discover just how pervasive the industries had been.

In the Lake District, oak and hazel were the main coppice crop, the former usually harvested every fifteen to eighteen years and the latter every ten or twelve years. Once the oak stems had been cut the bark was peeled and sent away for tanning leather. The stems were used to make bobbins and baskets, or cut into short sections, gathered into 'pitsteads' and burnt to make charcoal, which was then carted down to smelt-works on the lake shores. Charcoal was a vital resource: Arthur Ransome's *Swallows and Amazon* stories create a vivid picture of charcoal-burners and their families on the Coniston fells in the 1920s. It was a hard and singular life.

At the pitstead, piles of cut oak stems were gathered into a mound, then covered with soil. After lighting the middle of the pile the top was sealed and the wood allowed to burn very slowly, without burst-ing into flame. The 'earth-burn' could take several days and needed constant attention: too much heat or flame and the charcoal would be useless. These days it is easy to find old pitsteads, shelved clearings in the woods, decked with spring flowers in dappled sunshine, but there are no traditional charcoal-burners left and the fells are no longer wreathed in smoke.

The Smallwood Association sometimes organises special events in one or other of the Lakeland valleys, and it is possible then to see demon-strations of traditional crafts and catch a glimpse of how the work was done. The only current use for charcoal, produced in metal kilns, is for barbecues.

Having shown more than a passing inter-est in swill baskets and bobbins at craft stalls, it was inevitable that someone should have given me George Hogarth's phone number. Everyone said I should go and see him at work in the woods, down near Newby Bridge. But having acquired some experience of trying to find coppice-workers in the depths of southern forests, I made sure when I spoke to him that he gave me clear directions. He sounded helpful and it all seemed straightforward. The next day after an early drive I got to the gated track easily enough but then took half an hour going in circles through the wood: 'along the wide ride, left along another ride, and left again...' Eventually I realised I was into a new cut of coppice and there were stacks of poles and piles of brash-ings along the verge. The track opened out into a clearing and there was George Hogarth, splitting hazel stems outside his shelter.

It was a cloudy morning and by early afternoon there was heavy drizzle. Most of the photographs I took were fuzzy. I hardly wrote any notes, because we talked too much, and long afterwards all I could really remember was the green shade and the smell of the silky sap on the peeled oak stems. As I drove away two or three hours later, I realised I would never be able to find the place again.

Johnny Wood, beside the River Derwent near Rosthwaite. Like almost all the oakwoods of the Lake District, this was once an industrial site for the production of coppice-wood and charcoal. Now it is internationally recognised as a 'temperate rainforest', of special ecological interest.

Hazel coppice, ready to cut.

A block of felled woodland, recoppiced and regenerating after several decades of dereliction. Great Wood, near Keswick.

Bill Hogarth, fifty years a coppicer, making a besom in his woodland shelter near Newton Bridge. The wood provides a livelihood, in all weathers — but Bill always went home for dinner.

Splitting hazel stems for hurdles (stacked in the background). Bill Hogarth, finishing an order from a garden centre.

Bill Hogarth with a stack of oak stems. He had already stripped the bark and dispatched this to Devon, where it would be used to make tannin for preserving leather. The remaining stems were being loaded onto a truck to be made into garden furniture.

Charcoal-making the traditional way: Arthur Barker shovelling earth to seal a 'hot-spot' in a charcoal 'earth-burn', in the Coniston Woods near Brantwood. A burn of this sort might last for days, which is why, in the nineteenth century, whole families lived in wigwams around the pitsteads.

A metal charcoal kiln at work. The trick with charcoal is to keep out the oxygen and prevent rapid combustion, which would leave only ash.

Bill Hogarth's grandson, Neil, emptying the last few pieces of charcoal from a kiln in the woods near Newby Bridge. Neil was on a college placement to learn woodland skills, selling bags of barbecue charcoal at weekends.

There are still a lot of sensible uses for woodland produce. John Rudd of Dufton makes thousands of these garden rakes every year.

John Rudd in his workshop in Dufton. He has worked in a laith shop all his life, having learned the trade from his grandfather. Rakes are the same now as they were fifty years ago, except for the addition of a few iron nails. The teeth of the rake are made of birch, the head is ash and (according to John), the shaft is 'ramin'.

Shepherding is not a gentle occupation, and on the fells it is not often done at walking pace.
Judy Cubbey running right to keep sight of her dogs and cover the flank of a cut of sheep,
heading down from Watendlath Fell to the tarn. In the far distance is Skiddaw.

EIGHT

Watendlath Gather

There have been sheep on Watendlath Fell for a thousand years. The monks of Furness Abbey established one of their lucrative 'granges' here in the twelfth century, and through Medieval times a settlement of farms, clustered at the north end of the tarn, ran sheep and cattle on the unenclosed high fells. Crops were grown in open strips on the level ground around the tarn, with an encircling stone wall, called a ring garth, preventing the animals from eating the crops until after harvest-time. Gradually over the years a cob-webbing of drystone walls appeared further and further up the slopes. Some intakes were used for grazing, others were kept as woodland, or as bracken beds (for winter bedding).

Looking eastwards from the high fell at Jopplety How (a popular climb out of Borrowdale), Watendlath seems irresistibly pretty, but down the years it has had its share of failed harvests and bitter winters. There is only one working farm left, Old Fold, and it sustains one family, the Richardsons. Cattle still graze the intakes and sheep still roam the fells. When I was looking to follow a summer gather, Watendlath was one of the first places I thought of.

It was the end of June. I had driven up from Buxton and it was nearly dusk by the time I turned off the M6 for Keswick. I phoned Dick Richardson half hoping the forecast was bad and the shearing would be left for a day or two, but it was set fine and the gather would go ahead. Also, because it was likely to be a warm day, the team would start early – about 4am – to make sure the sheep were in the pens before it got too hot. There was no option if I wanted some pictures but to sleep in the car and be at Old Fold bright and early too.

The night was long and uncomfortable. At first light I stretched my legs by walking down to the Naddle Beck, its channels split into silver braids by tree roots and green-slate boulders. The water was low and the mud was drying fast, leaving heron tracks and beak-marks where oystercatchers had been out probing for freshwater-mussels. I followed the beck downstream, looking for signs of otter. By the time I got back to the car, Castlerigg Stone Circle was aglow with golden sunshine and I was half an hour late.

At Old Fold, Shaun Richardson and Judy Cubbey, a shepherdess from Seatoller, were already setting out with their dogs, Nip, Josie, Sam, Foxy, Peg and Floss. I walked with them south along the walled track and over Bleatarn Gill, then followed Judy up to gather the Dock Tarn heaf. It was hot by 7am, and the dogs were slow ('they need a boot up the arse to make 'em ga'). By contrast, the sheep were quick. Tempers were soon frayed. Eventually the mixed heaf of Herdwicks and Swaledales was gathered into tens and twenties, then worked downhill over the boulder slopes and through the bracken banks. There is far more bracken in the Lake District than there used to be: on some farms the dogs are now trained to bark, so shepherds will know exactly where they are when working through dense forests of fronds. But on most farms shepherds still like their dogs to be silent, to listen for commands.

After a couple of hours the cut of sheep was off the fell, through the intake and along the walled track, then into the pens at Watendlath. There was dust everywhere, including all over me and my camera. I knew the splintered light would make the last few photographs more dramatic, but I also knew I had missed the pictures I most wanted from the fells. The problem had been trying to work into the light, and as usual the sheep had moved too quickly and too erratically on the ridges for me to get into a good position. For a few minutes, all the effort in getting to Old Fold seemed to have been wasted. Everyone was in a bad mood; even the dogs were snappy. I had a cup of tea and talked to Dick. The biggest gather of the year was to be next morning, when the Top End heaf was brought down from Coldbarrow. It would be another hot day, another early start. I thought about it for a few moments but there was really no decision to be made: if I wanted the pictures I would have to work for them.

I drove home over the Alston moors that afternoon with stiff limbs and a weary heart, but was up next morning at 3.30 and back on the fell by 5.30. The light was softer, and the atmosphere heavy. I was still tired, but this time I made the right choice in circling west and south, climbing high above the Watendlath valley. My notebook, terse as ever, described the gather:

Main ridge, Top End, funnelling into the valley. More sheep than yesterday. Light flatter. Warm/hazy. David Tyson on the ridge crest, to stop sheep getting too far ahead. Dick also on near side. Both spent a lot of time standing looking. Far away, could see Shaun and the Blands (Stuart and son Johnny, acting as runner) shifting the dogs and working the streams of sheep into the valley. Came together below us. Circled down behind them: followed them in. A good gather, half the time of yesterday and four times the sheep. Lots of dogs: a ruck at the back, chasing strays. Midges and clegs very bad (Dick calls them 'horse-bees').

I got one good photograph, grabbed in an instant as a score of Swaledales burst past Dick Richardson. He was holding a lost lamb and behind him was the flattened wall of the east ridge, towards Shivery Knott.

When I spoke to Dick recently about this late-June gather of 1995 he remembered it well, because the weather had been like the summers of his childhood. Blue remembered hills: horse-bees at harvest: skylarks around the pummyfold.

Once onto the walled track east of Watendlath Tarn the hard part of the gather is done, and it is just a matter of keeping the sheep moving. By now even the dogs are in a playful mood and are more interested in tussling with each other than driving the sheep.

It is about 7am and already hot. In the pens at Old Fold the dust rises as the sheep are separated for shearing by Shaun Richardson and Judy Cubbey. The sheep are a mixed bunch of Herdwick and Swaledale (according to Dick Richardson, 'Swaddles' all have a bit of Herdwick in them: good sheep, but not so sturdy as the pure Herdwicks).

The packhorse Bridge at Watendlath.

Watendlath from the path to High Tove. Old Fold Farm is to the top left of the picture, beyond the sheep pens. The National Trust car park is filling up: visitors either make for the open fells or for the little tearoom, hidden in the trees on the right.

The Coldbarrow gather, with a big cut of sheep heading off the fell, down towards Watendlath.

David Tyson on the ridge near Black Knott, checking for any sheep turning west.

The sheep are still moving fast down the slope to Bleatarn Gill. Dick Richardson has picked up a stray lamb, lost in the confusion. The gather started at about 4 am, and it is now about 6.30. The sun has risen over Middle Crag and High Tove, but the shadows are still long.

Dick Richardson, still carrying a stray lamb, follows the drift of sheep down through the intake at Lingy West Side, towards Watendlath.

By now it is another hot day, and David Tyson has dispensed with his coat. Ash pollards line the lane.

After the gather: about eight o'clock at the Old Fold pens. Visitors at the adjacent National Trust car park are probably wondering if farmers just stand around all day talking.

Side Farm and its cluster of barns and outbuildings, from the old slate quarry at the foot of Place Fell. In the middle distance, across the level pastureland of Patterdale, is Ullswater. Helvellyn is covered in mist to the top left of the picture. A typical November day in the Lake District.

NINE

Patterdale Sheep Pens

For a short time, I felt I knew the Lake District quite well: not just its wildlife and landscapes, but its people too. Doing interpretive projects for both the National Trust and the National Park Authority allowed me to share different sides of conversations about farming, access and conservation.

Down the years, tenant farmers have often regarded their landlords with a healthy mixture of cynical disdain and grudging respect. Times have changed and many hill farmers have had to get used to dealing with land agents representing banking syndicates and bankrupt viscounts. In the Lake District, the relationship is more complex. Most of the land in the mountainous core of the National Park is owned by the National Trust, and has been so for a generation. The Trust seeks to conserve the landscape through sustainable and traditional farming methods, but it also likes to make money.

Some of the Trust's estate managers and wardens, who are far more professional than they were a decade ago, view farming as a management tool: a way to sustain the sort of landscape people want to see. This means they have no time for bad farming practice or for some of the 'characters' who lease the Trust's properties. On the other hand the Trust attracts and manages grants from all sorts of national and European agencies to support conservation work and the local community. So if a farmer wants to improve his or her standard of living, his best approach is to take the money from ESA/Stewardship/Enhancement schemes and diversify, to take on other part-time employment or create a B+B or tea-room business.

The result of all this is that the tenant/landlord relationship has come full circle: Lake District farmers have a healthy disdain for the Trust, because it is mean/greedy/wrong-headed, tempered by a grudging respect, because it is supportive/forward-thinking/fights its corner. By way of contrast, the National Park Authority owns very little land, processes planning applications, administers rights of way, and is still charged with trying to support the local community. Thus, farmers' attitudes to the National Park are usually dismissive or hostile.

The north-east corner of the Lake District includes some little-visited fells and hidden waters – places to keep quiet about because they still have a sense of space about them. But there are also some very popular honeypots, and of these the Ullswater/Patterdale valley, from Pooley Bridge to the Kirkstone Pass, is the busiest. Visitors like to potter along the shore looking for Wordsworth's daffodils, stroll up to Aira Force, take a steamer cruise or climb Striding Edge to Helvellyn. There is something for everyone, and people have been coming here for a very long time.

This means that farming in the area has become a half-hidden or clandestine operation: moving tractors along the roads early in the morning to avoid traffic: keeping belligerent tups away from footpaths: not speaking to walkers because you'd never get any work done otherwise. A few years ago, local people around Glenridding regarded visitors as a necessary evil. Now they see them as a business opportunity.

I have fond memories of camping with my family near Watermillock in 1990. We took the steamer over to Howtown to do a circular walk back to the Aira Force car park. The best moment of this for me was seeing the beautiful birch woods near Silver Point, but for everyone else the best bit was buying an ice cream at Side Farm.

A few years later I was contracted by the National Trust to work with the Taylforth family of Side Farm, to create display panels for their new tea-room. I took some photographs and talked with them about how they thought life had changed, but in essence it had not: they were still making ends meet by working the farm and providing facilities for tourists. This approach had been adopted by Mike Taylforth when he moved here in 1962 with his wife Dulcie (of Hartsop). Between them they had opened a campsite, pony-trekking centre and a little shop, at the side of the farmhouse where the footpath turns down to cross the Goldrill Beck in Patterdale.

When I asked Mike about how they had approached the business, and what they would say to the next generation, he had a motto all ready: 'Look after the farm and it'll look after you. But do something new every year.' These days Mike is retired and it is son and daughter-in-law, Robin and Anthea, who run Side Farm. They have diversified: Robin is a contract shearer and scanner, Andrea runs a signing business and is a retained firefighter. The tea-room will be a success because they will make it work. Not because they like people or hours of extra work, but because they know that is the only way to survive. I never got the feeling with either Mike or Robin that they would have tolerated a photographer dogging their heels if it had not been for the greater good of the farm.

I spent two autumn days following cuts of Swaledale sheep down from the fells to Side Farm, covering the same ground I had got to know in the 1980s when I was writing a walking guide. This time I could not stop to identify fungi in the birch woods or enjoy the cloud-breaks over Fairfield and Catstye Cam. Shepherds and photographers often miss pretty sunsets: the work concentrates or narrows the mind. I was focused instead on how the sheep were worked into the pens, to be sorted and sent out again for tupping.

It was a dull, mild afternoon, the sort that people forget when they talk about how beautiful the fells can be at the back end of the year. After the gather and shedding I spent a few minutes looking around the farmyard, the hub of any day's work. The cluster of buildings leading into it had all had a different purpose in their heyday. Keeping such structures intact is a headache for the National Trust as well as for their tenants: most buildings are too small to be functional.

The new tea-room at Side Farm had been the tack room for the stables, and on either side of it were 'hulls' or small 'boxes' used for calves or pigs. Across the yard was a big eighteenth century bank barn, which once housed a byre for eight cattle and a stable for three working horses. Opposite this was a midden shed, where dung had been kept for later spreading on the hayfields. It was impossible now to tell if any of these buildings was still in use at all: the only signs of life were the polypod fern growing all over the shed roof, and the green and red plastic dumper-truck that Joe Taylforth had pedalled into the midden yard.

Andrea Taylforth putting away the tool-kit in the midden shed at Side Farm. The boys' vehicles are parked up behind the gatepost. The climate in this part of Cumbria is wet and windy – hence the ferns, and the 'crow-steps' to keep the roof on.

The Taylforth family: Robin, Andrea, Sam and Joe, with dogs Jock and Fred.

An autumn sheep gather, down towards the Ullswater shore from Patterdale Common. The sun is dipping below Helvellyn in the early afternoon.

A cut of sheep (mainly Swaledale) heading for home. Robin Taylforth and Robert Wear at the back with the dogs.

Sheep pens at Herrimans, close to the main buildings at Side Farm. The old barn in the background is used to store hay or feed. In the foreground is the dipping shed; next to this is a sheep shed. Bales of silage are stored on the far side of the yard. The sheep (Swaledales and Cheviots) are being sorted into groups of forty or fifty at a time, to be sent out again with a tup.

Mike and Robin Taylforth shedding (ie separating) sheep at Harrimans. The gate can be swung either way, to left or right, sending the sheep into separate paddocks.

The gathering team at Side Farm: Robert Wear, Mike Taylforth, Alan Wear, Robin Taylforth and Eric Wear. Farming neighbours rely on each other when they need shepherding help. At other times, such as silage-making or shearing, they usually rely on contract labour.

Andrew Ivinson in the sheep pens at Beckside Farm, at Sandwick on the south shore of Ullswater. Sheep make attractive hosts for internal parasites, and they also need mineral supplements. But they do not like the taste of the dose and have to have it dispensed into the backs of their mouths.

Out from the pens at Beckside: Hardwicks ready and eager to be back on the fell.

Monty and Jock pulling a double-breasted plough, raising drills to sow turnips on First Low Field, Sillywrea Farm. Black-headed gulls, on the look-out for earthworms, follow behind John Dodd's back.

TEN

Clean Money

At the headland of First Low Field the horses turned again and John Dodd pushed down hard on the stilts of the drill-plough to lift the share clear of the soil. Once into line and ready, he pulled on the traces to raise the horses' heads:

Head up… steady now, steady. Woa…woa!
Get up a step: just a step at a time, Monty.
Steady… steady… Jee-up!

And off they went, ploughing the last break or acre-strip of what would be the turnip field.

The turnip transformed British farming in the eighteenth century. Until then, most sheep and cattle were slaughtered in the early winter because there was not enough hay or straw to see them through. People lived on salt beef, smoked lamb and carrots, if they were lucky. With the arrival of the turnip (from Holland) most farms were able to tide over their stock and have them in good condition for the spring. This went on for more than two centuries, until the advent of silage.

There's nothing looks nicer than a straight-drilled field, and nothing worse than a twisted one.

Once the field had been harrowed the double mound-board made a tidy job of turning each break into a patch of velvet-brown corduroy. The horses were well-matched. Monty, the old roan, had wilful days when he deliberately pushed too fast or stopped half way down a row. Just now he was going well beside Jim, the young bay. Stride for stride, a step at a time. Keeping the drills straight was John's only worry. As he worked he watched the mark made by the previous row, guiding the plough to compensate for uneven ground or a drift to left or right. Jim, in the furrow, had an easy hoof-guide, but Monty, on the 'land' side, had nothing to follow and might have drifted had it not been for the long stick or bar put on in place of the usual rope-cord to link bridles.

Steady… woah! Woa-ho!
Back… back! Come in, come in now… J'up!

It took a day to raise the drills, a full day with the usual break at just after midday for the horses to rest and take some hay. In the middle of the afternoon a flock of gulls began to gather until there were forty or fifty following the plough. They were black-headed gulls, adults in full breeding plumage, and they followed tight behind John's back like a flurry of giant snowflakes. The earth was dry and when the job was finished the birds were soon gone, drifting over the valley to the east and leaving the field still and bare.

The sowing would be done in the next two or three days. The month was already half gone; John had left the soft turnips to give the young horses some work, to keep them fit before the hay-making of June or July. Although soft turnips and the new stubble turnips could be put in late, the usual time for swedes was mid-May. 'Better in by Hiring Day', which was the 13th, the long-forgotten mark in the year when

Jock the young Clydesdale at work thinning and gapping turnips, but very interested in what is happening in the rest of the countryside.

John's grandfather would have joined all the local farmers at the Hiring Fair.

Sillywrea Farm may seem old fashioned in its use of horses, but in other ways it is ahead of its time – or perhaps the wheel of farming has come full circle. Sustainability is one of the watchwords in countryside stewardship and agricultural policy, and it lies behind most of what John Dodd does on his two hundred acres. His income is based on sheep and cattle – on what the store and fat animals bring at market. Only bulls and tups are bought in, to reduce inbreeding and keep the stock healthy. All other replacements are born and raised on the farm, fed on grass, hay, barley, straw and turnips, all grown on the farm. The fertility in the land comes from generous helpings of manure, with just a little Potash or Phosphate for the tillage.

'What goes out is clean money: there's not a lot coming against it. If I had more livestock and was selling more, I'd have to buy more feedstuff. Whereas my feed bills aren't big: a little for the ewes at lambing time and oats for the horses.'

John says that if the farm suffered because of his insistence on using horses he would get rid of them, but so far there has been no need for agonizing decisions – John loves his horses and I do not believe he would ever do without them. As long as everything is done in season it hardly matters how long it takes, if you enjoy the work. Sillywrea's 200 acres is made up of fifteen fields and a little oak wood. Most of the land is grass: pasture and haymeadow. Only about 30 acres is tillage, based on a five year rotation (barley, barley, turnips, barley, grass).

I kept a notebook when I was photographing the horse work at Sillywrea. I started in the middle of summer, so some of the earliest work was with the barley:

17th August
Phone call from Mrs Dodd: 'They've got a start.'

5.30. Combining winter barley. Stormy sky: sunshine then heavy shower and thunder: a 'catchy' day. There's wicken (couch) in the barley, so John may spray for next crop on Thackey field.
Grain bagged and into loft by 7.00.
Still a fierce sky – slanting rays through stormclouds. Stoat working the edge of the road by the quarry.

20th August
Fat lambs to mart: saw them away at about 8.00. Then up to see checking of cattle on Quarry Field. Barley-straw baled. Swallows flying low over pastures in watery sunshine.

21st August
Leading straw. Evening still and sunny. Wispy clouds edged gold and peach as light failed. Half moon over Harsondale. Flocks of rooks on spring barley: John putting out the scarer for morning. Straw going into galvanised shed and cow byre (cattle out till Christmas).
Hay and straw for the farm: it goes back into the land rather than away: ('There's one thing worse than buying hay and straw, and that's selling it').
Out to Thackey for final load. Dusk cyanine and silver.

29th August.
Dew on fields/autumn in the air. Warm muggy day.
All morning on the Thackey: John ploughing and harrowing stubble with Monty and Jim. Through the morning, twelve yards ('three rows of plough equals a good yard' – measured by strides). So, will all be finished today.
The horses getting lazy and awkward in the hot weather. Monty going too briskly and getting hot again.
Swallows hawking over fields and into the barns.

In a fortnight the first of the new barley would be sown and the tup sales would be under way. Everything on the farm could be measured by the tilt of the earth, the passing of the seasons.

Hand hoeing turnips on First Low Field. After the horse-hoe has finished its work it is left to John Dodd to take out any weeds close to or between the plants. A hard job, to be done a little at a time.

Jim scuffling turnips: light work for a young horse.

Above: *Clamping turnips at Sillywrea Farm on a chill day in early winter. Monty the roan Clydesdale never looks happy, whatever the weather.*

Left: *Frost on the turnips: ready to top and lead.*

Above: *Seedcorn ready for sowing.*

Right: *Emptying seed into the drill hopper. Winter barley for the Thackey Field, Sillywrea Farm.*

A shimmering field of barley. Sillywrea Farm aims to be self-sufficient in winter fodder: grain, turnips and hay.

Combine harvester cutting barley at Sillywrea. The combine extracts the grain and leaves behind the chaff and straw, which will be baled later. A bright but 'catchy' day: rain is closing in from the north.

Scottie waits patiently while John and David fit straw bales into the barn, next to the farmhouse at Sillywrea.

A new Clydesdale foal at Sillywrea Farm. John Dodd with Dick: nine months old and looking nervous. 'Hardly quite a foal – more like a yearling,' said John, who already knew Dick was going to be a good 'un.

ELEVEN

Horse Talk

Horse sales were important dates in the farming year, to be ringed in pencil on the calendar, whether you needed a new foal or not. A century ago every farm had its working horses, and there was a constant turnover of Shires, Clydesdales, Percherons and Punches. The end really came in the 1940s, but at the time nobody inside or outside the industry realised where tractors and mechanisation could lead us. For their part, most farmers embraced efficiency if it meant less effort and more income, but they also missed their horses. 'If things were bad, you could always talk to your horse' was a phrase I heard several times when I was talking to old labourers about their days on the land.

Heavy horses seem to occupy the same sort of niche in British culture as steam trains; their passing marked the end of a Golden Age. In 1900, there were over a million horses on British farms; by 1939 this was down to less than 700,000, and in 1958 the total had shrunk to just 80,000. Since then, there have been too few working horses to warrant an official count. But like so much in the countryside, things are not so straightforward as they seem; the rise of horse power in the late eighteenth century had been as dramatic as its subsequent demise. And we do not lament the passing of oxen from our fields.

In the autumn of 1992 I went to one of the regular Horse Sales at Wigton to get a flavour of what things might have been like, and to meet up with John Dodd of Sillywrea Farm, who was looking for a foal. At the time I was keen to follow John's working year, because he was the only farmer I knew who still relied on horses, and I was concerned that he might soon retire or buy himself a tractor. However,

as I write this in 2004, John has done neither and his daughter and son-in-law (Frances and David Wise) show every sign of resisting mechanical temptation.

The horse sale was a mixed affair. In the morning I watched horses being paraded before judging along the isle of the open-sided sheds: all looked immaculate with their heads up and their tails decked in ribbons and straw plaits. But when it came to the sale the crowd was thin, and not one of the first nine Clydesdale fillies in the ring made its reserve.

David liked the look of one foal. When I asked him why, he smiled shyly and said 'It's not a good colour, but it's got a friendly face. John will know if it will turn out all right.' When I asked John he just said: 'A good horse is never a bad colour', but although he stood through the afternoon at the sale ring, he kept his hands in his pockets. Later, I saw him talking to a horseman from Carlisle – a character with a wrinkled nut-brown face and long whiskers, smoking a broken-off pipe, with his hands tucked into a broad leather belt over a blue boiler-suit. 'A serious fellow altogether,' said John afterwards, with a twinkle in his eye. But he bought a foal from the man, and that was the real business of the day.

Breaking a horse was a skilled task in husbandry. It took about a month and cost about £20 (plus hay and corn) in the early 1900s. The average farm wage at the time was about 30 shillings (£1.50) a week; a farmer could not afford a horse with bad habits, so the breaker was worth his extra wages. I asked John Dodd how long it would take for him to break his new foal and he reckoned about three months, starting when it was about two and a half years old. He took a long time because he had to fit it around other work, but I also think John enjoyed working with his horses. It was no hardship to put in extra hours and days.

The first thing I do is bring them into the stable, turn them wrong way on into the stall and tie them from each stall post, so they're tied from each side of the head, and I put the breaking harness on them. And I give them half a day tied that way so they can get used to the feel of the harness. The second day I'll put them into the loose box and let them get out and walk about so they can feel the harness. They get over any twitchiness and jumping. The third day I'll take them out for a walk, to quiet them in traffic, and then I'll lunge them... This goes on for about a month... Then I'll drive the horse backwards and forwards in a field. Then the ploughing harness, and yoke them to a log or other heavy object, so they know they're pulling something. Then work it double, with another horse. Then with chains, and back into the stall for a cart harness, and lunge them again, to get used to the rattle. Then fasten them into the stalls for a few days with shafts on. This goes on day and day about for three months.

John usually starts breaking a new horse in January, so it can work its way through the various skills it will need in its working life.

After they've had a hard day working turnip land or raising drills, and they come in pretty tired, I'll just slip them into the mowing machine, drop the bar down and slip into gear and go round the yard. They're practically turning in a circle all the time and I rattle them round the yard, first one way and then the other.

The first time I visited Sillywrea Farm, John was working with one of his oldest horses, called Winston. Winston looked calm and placid, but apparently this had not been the case when John had bought him:

I thought he was very cheap and I bought him off a dealer when he was three and a half. He'd run an extra year, so naturally he was big and powerful. The dealer was honest... I asked if the horse had been 'touched', but he said the horse had only been halter-broken. But after I made a start to break him I wasn't so sure. I got the impression that someone had tried to break him but given it up as a bad job. He had such a fear when you said 'Woa' to him: he just tensed up and bucked or pulled, and went round and round. The first time I put him into the long reins, well... I was pleased to get him back into the stable. He was a hard horse to break...

I knew when we put Winston into the shafts that there would be a carry on with him. I got three other good men to help. One I knew, Jack Huddlestone, had been a horse-breaker. He had the horse at one side of the head and I had him at the other, and there was one man at the reins and another had a rope from him. Funnily enough we got him yoked into the roller and he was just like an old'un: he never moved. Quiet as anything and we set off. He went about 5 yards and then, by Jove, he went away, and quite honestly he was carrying the four of us. But we kept him going: he'd been working all day from about six, and we took him in about half past nine. We couldn't turn him into the field that night!

A couple of days later three of us put him into the roller again, and he was a lot better. More relaxed. Then he made the awfulest jump and his great feet came up past my head. Jack, the other side, had been picking up bits of rough straw and throwing them onto his back, and they'd been getting stuck behind the cart saddle. Jack never told me. We laughed about it later, and he said 'I knew sooner or later that horse was going to bolt. If he'd bolted when you were on your own you wouldn't have had a chance. I thought it was a bad job if three of us couldn't stop him... If you stop them the first time, they're never as keen to try the second!'

Adolescent and enjoying his freedom: Dick at eighteen months. Sillywrea Farm.

The forgotten art of horse-breaking. Dick, the young Clydesdale at Sillywrea Farm, being 'lunged' by John Dodd. 'You stand in the middle and let them trot around in a circle. It's the easiest way to get them exercised and tired. The trick is to teach them to trot both ways, or they turn one-sided.'

John and Jock (half-brother to Dick), gapping turnips. John is having to wait for the young horse, who has grabbed a mouthful of grass from the headland on the way round.

Monty scratching.

Ploughing the lea: Clydesdales Jock and Jim working up the slope of Lane Foot.

Above: *Learning the trade: Richard Wise helping his grandfather drive in the ploughing team.*

Right: *Heading for home: Jim, wet and muddy after scuffling turnips. John Dodd has hooked his jacket onto the horse's hames and is checking how much work is left for morning.*

At the end of the day: John Dodd with Richard, who has waited up in his pyjamas to see his grand-dad and Jim back to the stable.

Selling tack from a horse box, Appleby Fair.

TWELVE

Appleby Fair

Towards the end of May each year I hear gypsy caravans passing my garden on the Allendale Road in Hexham, as they start the climb westwards over the Pennines. Often, it is early in the morning, and I lie in bed listening as they clatter past the window. They have probably come a long way, and they still have a long way to go. It may have taken them a fortnight to get this far, and they will stop off again two or three times at village greens and lay-bys from Alston and Melmerby to Langwathby. But by whatever road they go, they all arrive in early June at Appleby in the Eden Valley.

Appleby Fair is a medieval relic, preserved by Royal Charter for the 'purchase and sale of all manner of goods, cattle, horses, mares, geldings'. Horse-trading has always been its key purpose, and it has survived because of the Romany love affair with horses. Although the event attracts thousands of visitors there is nothing very much to do during the day, unless you are buying, selling, showing, racing, or talking horses. People mill about along the muddy tracks of what was once Gallows Hill, looking for a focal point or centrepiece, but there isn't one: the event is run by and for travellers, and all they are interested in is their horses.

This was a refreshing change. I took my camera into quiet corners of Fair Hill where men with rumpled suits and floral shirts talked in whispers with other men in rumpled suits and floral shirts, casting glances over piebald and skewbald horses of no aesthetic merit. After a very short while I realised that the bartering was a private affair, and that unless I was looking for a thick ear I should mind my own business.

One traveller I had chatted with a few days before at Melmerby avoided me by tripping backwards over a fence and re-tying his shoe-lace in a hurry. He was giving me time to get back among the tourists and take pictures of pretty wagons, decorative tack and Crown Derby porcelain. I took the hint and wandered down the dealing lane, side-stepping heaps of dung. Every few minutes there was a commotion as a horse and racing buggy parted the crowd, the driver perched on a flimsy frame and barely in control of the beast in front of him. Harness racing is a passion among travellers, along with BMWs and gold.

After an hour or two on the hill I walked back into Appleby, which in normal times is a pretty little town on a twist of the River Eden. Local pubs were doing great trade, but everyone else was keeping out of the way. The Eden was picturesque as always, and downstream of the bridge there were boys and girls leading horses in and out of the water, swimming them in the shallows and scrubbing them with washing-up liquid before leading them back to the fair. The banks of the river were lined with people enjoying themselves, asking no more than a view of the horses. It was a beautiful day and a grand spectacle.

Inevitably, some local people want Appleby Fair closed, because it creates havoc, fosters bad behaviour and adds little to the economy. But anything worth keeping comes at a price. I came away grateful to have avoided pick-pockets, fights and horse stampedes. The photographs I had taken hardly reflected the magic of the event, and perhaps the magic was in my mind, but I was happy to have been there, and happier still to know that such uncompromising oddities can survive through changing times.

A week or so after my visit to Appleby Fair, when the gypsy wagons were clattering past my garden on their way home, I asked John Dodd of Sillywrea Farm if he had ever employed travellers as seasonal workers. Sixty or seventy years ago, farming relied on itinerant or migrant labourers, often Irish, who worked for half the year on English farms, a month here a month there, before returning home to tend to their own smallholdings. John had fond memories of some of them – good and reliable workers who returned year after year. Of the travellers he was less forthcoming, I think because they were true drifters and could not be relied on to do an honest day's work.

However, there is an overgrown trackway half a mile from John's farm, next to the Carts Bog pub at the road junction below Stublick Moor, where gypsies always used to camp. John remembers when he was a boy, sneaking away from home on summer evenings to sit around their fires and listen to their stories about far away places, and horses. Always horses.

The old track where the gypsies used to camp is now fenced off, but in late May there are always two or three caravans and colourful wagons parked nearby on the road verge, as if to stake a spiritual claim to the open road.

There is a famous clip from the TV comedy classic Only Fools and Horses *where Del is trying to play it cool and leans on a bar counter that is suddenly not there. This picture reminds me of that moment. The Clydesdale stallion is being looked over by potential purchasers, who are trying to appear cool. Perhaps the fence wire gave way a moment after the picture was taken, at Appleby Horse Fair.*

Travelling farrier working quickly at his anvil: Appleby Fair.

Fitting the shoe: the hot metal is burned into the hoof of the piebald gelding and for a few moments the air is full of acrid smoke.

Visitors clear a path for a horse and buggy. Two worlds almost collide.

Caravans as far as the eye can see, some decorative and others less so. Family fun and fortune-telling.

Washing horses in the Eden. Big crowds gather to watch the horses being brought down to be washed and groomed in the shallows.